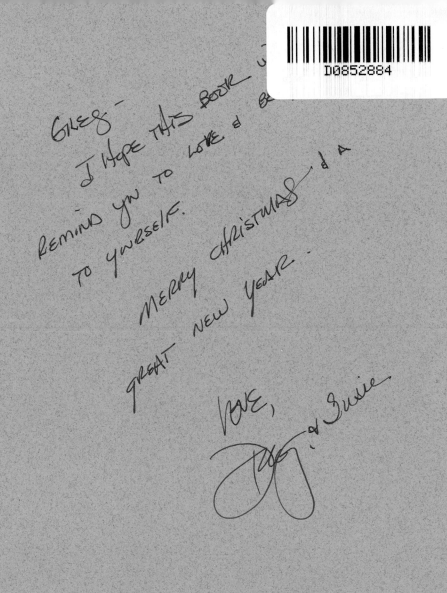

Greg -
I hope this book w
reminds you to love & be
to yourself.

Merry Christmas d a
great new year.

Love,
Peg & Suzie

HEAL
YOUR SOUL,
HEAL
THE WORLD

November 28, 1998

May my newest book bring
inspiration to every part of
your life!

Best always,
June Cotner

Also by June Cotner

Bless the Day:
Prayers and Poems to Nurture Your Soul

Bedside Prayers:
Prayers and Poems for When You Rise and Go to Sleep

Graces: Prayers & Poems for Everyday Meals
and Special Occasions

The Home Design Handbook: The Essential Planning Guide
for Building, Buying, or Remodeling a Home

HEAL
YOUR SOUL,
HEAL
THE WORLD

Prayers and Poems to Comfort, Inspire,
and Connect Humanity

JUNE COTNER

Andrews McMeel
Publishing

Kansas City

www.andrewsmcmeel.com

98 99 00 01 02   BVG   10 9 8 7 6 5 4 3 2 1

Library of Congress Cataloging-in-Publication Data
Heal your soul, heal the world : prayers and poems to comfort, inspire, and connect humanity / [selected by] June Cotner.

    p.   cm.
  Includes index.
  ISBN 0-8362-6915-2 hd
  1. Religious poetry, American.   2. Prayers.   I. Cotner, June, 1950–   .
PS595.R4H4   1998
811.008'0382—dc21   98-22359
                                                                 CIP

Design by Mauna Eichner
Illustrations by Tanya Maiboroda

In your light I learn how to love.
In your beauty, how to make poems.

You dance inside my chest,
where no one sees you,

but sometimes I do, and that
sight becomes this art.

RUMI
(1207—1273)
TRANSLATED BY COLEMAN BARKS

CONTENTS

3
....

FORGIVENESS

4
....

COMPASSION

5
....

SPIRITUALITY

6

NATURE AND THE ENVIRONMENT

9

COMMUNITY AND WORLDLY CONCERNS

10

WONDER AND APPRECIATION

1 1

PRAISE AND CELEBRATION

1 2

TOLERANCE

1 3

HOPE FOR THE FUTURE

1 4

INSPIRATION

A LETTER TO READERS

Heal Your Soul, Heal the World is a book that has grown in my soul for many years, probably evolving from the time I contemplated the stars as a teenager and sensed a universal connection with everyone and everything in the world. As a young adult, my growing reverence for nature was nurtured by many years of backpacking, an activity I still enjoy today. I have always felt a sense of reciprocity with the natural environment. If I took care of the forest, the forest would take care of me.

In the late 1980s, I was inspired by my acquaintance with the late Danaan Perry, founder of Earthstewards Network. In 1990, I attended the Earth and Spirit Conference (sponsored by the Chinook Learning Community, now the Whidbey Institute), not knowing where that participation would take me. As I developed as a writer, ideas from that powerful conference have led to the framework of this book.

In the process of creating my earlier spiritual poetry anthologies, *Graces*, *Bedside Prayers*, and *Bless the Day*, I received many wonderful submissions that didn't fit the themes of these books. However, many of the selections reflected the universal connection I experienced as a teenager. Of all my projects, *Heal Your Soul, Heal the World* is the book I feel will be my most important legacy.

At the deepest level, we're aware that what each of us does makes a difference in the world. Just as we observe the ripples from a pebble thrown into a pond, we sense that even something as simple as a smile or a kind word has a similar effect somewhere in our world. I recently experienced an unexpected reminder that a kind word affects the world better than a harsh one. I came upon a young mother who was yelling at her child in a public rest room and threatening to spank her if she didn't behave. While my initial instinct was to protect the child, I said to the mother, "Some days can be really tough, can't they?" Immediately the mother broke down and between tears told me she had just learned that she had cancer. I came away from that situation determined to view others with more compassion and a willingness to "see" behind the apparent scene.

The individual challenges we face at our soul levels, whether it be in our home, at work, or in our community, provide the greatest raw resource for global change—far and beyond what we reasonably should expect politicians or corporate regulators to do for us. While it is important to "think global," it is even more imperative that we "act local"—to borrow a bumper-sticker phrase. That's what *Heal Your Soul, Heal the World* is all about. What we do at the dinner table each night is more critical than the letter we write to our senator.

The toughest challenge in completing *Heal Your Soul, Heal the World* was knowing that many excellent selections would not be published due to the ultimate page length of the book. I have a substantial start on a possible volume two and am currently accepting submissions. If you feel inspired after reading this book, please send favorite selections to the address below. Typed copies are always appreciated (with your name, address, and phone number at the top of each page). If you include a self-addressed stamped envelope, you'll eventually receive a reply. I hope to hear from you!

June Cotner
P.O. Box 2765
Poulsbo, WA 98370

THANKS

I'M MOST GRATEFUL TO Patty Rice, senior editor at Andrews McMeel Publishing, for immediately recognizing and appreciating the potential for *Heal Your Soul, Heal the World: Prayers and Poems to Comfort, Inspire, and Connect Humanity*. Also, I value the terrific support received from the staff at Andrews McMeel: Hugh Andrews, national sales director/book division, Jay Hyde, director of marketing, Shannon Guder, publicist, and Jennifer Fox, editorial assistant. As always, I'm enormously grateful to my agent, Denise Marcil, for finding the perfect house for this book and for her constant support and encouragement.

Beginning with my first anthology, *Graces*, I used a test-market group to evaluate the selections in each of my anthologies to help determine the final content of each book. I believe this process has helped create books that appeal to people of all faiths and beliefs and are accessible to general readers. Usually my test-market group consists of twenty individuals, but so many people expressed genuine excitement for *Heal Your Soul, Heal the World* that the test-market group consisted of thirty-two individuals representing many spiritual and religious beliefs, including a priest, a rabbi, a minister, three editors, several family members, many dear friends, and ten poets.

Specifically, I would like to thank each member of my test-market group: Father Paul Keenan (author of *Good News for Bad Days: Living a Soulful Life* and cohost of the national ABC radio program, *Religion on the Line*), Rabbi Rami M. Shapiro (storyteller, poet, author of *Minyan: Ten Principles for Living a Life of Integrity* and four other books), and Reverend Gary W. Huffman (coauthor of *The Bible: A to Z* and pastor of First Presbyterian Church, PCUSA, Shelbyville, Indiana). These three spiritual leaders rated many selections in almost an identical manner, which to me reflects our experience of the same universal spirit, regardless of religious beliefs.

My editor, Patty Rice, and her editorial assistant, Jennifer Fox, took time out of their very busy schedules to offer feedback on *Heal Your Soul, Heal the World*. Joyce Standish, an independent editor with her own company ("papers" in Las Vegas, Nevada) volunteered her time to this effort. I have greatly appreciated Joyce's editorial feedback, astute revisions, and wonderful encouragement over many years.

Deepest thanks goes to my husband, Jim Graves; my daughter, Kirsten Cotner Myrvang; my son, Kyle Myrvang; and my cousin, Margie Cotner Potts for providing such valuable feedback on the manuscript. And where would any writer be without the support of terrific friends? I'm so grateful to count the following people as dear friends who gave so freely of their time to critique a very lengthy manuscript: Lynn Eathorne Bradley, Jennifer Jane Callen, Patty Forbes Cheng, Judy Denney, Sue Gitch, Deborah Ham, Patricia Huckell, Charlotte Carter Izett, Susan Peterson, and Ron Sharp.

The process of creating spiritual poetry anthologies has brought many wonderful poets into my life. The following poets enthusiastically agreed to critique the manuscript, and many of them thought of ways to make great poems even better. Genuine gratitude goes to the following poets: Janine Canan (author of *She Rises Like the Sun: Invocations of the Goddess* and seven other books), Kelly Cherry (author of *Natural Theology*, *God's Loud Hand*, and ten other books), Barbara Crooker (prolific poet and winner of many poetry awards), Maureen Tolman Flannery (author of *Secret of the Rising Up: Poems of Mexico*), Penny

Harter (author of *Turtle Blessing* and *Lizard Light: Poems from the Earth* and thirteen other books), Margaret Anne Huffman (award-winning journalist, author of *Through the Valley: Prayers for Violent Times* and seventeen other books), Arlene Gay Levine (author of *39 Ways to Open Your Heart*), Shirley Kobar (published in *Between the Heartbeats* and four of my anthologies), Elizabeth Searle Lamb (author of *Today and Every Day*), and Paul Nelson (cofounder of the NW Spokenword LAB in Auburn, Washington, www.splab.org).

Pulling double duty critiquing the manuscript were my two employees Tricia Treacy (who also secured permissions) and Kim Langevin (who did most of the data entry). Also, I'd like to thank Ginelle McCall for helping out with word processing, Cheryl Edmondson and John Wood for editorial suggestions, Shawna Sitton for proofreading, Kevin Jennings for his computer expertise, and Roger Block for general all-around support.

For the poets who did not make the final cut for this book, I'd like to thank you for the contribution your words have made to my life. I trust your fine poems will find a home someday, so that others can appreciate the wisdom and beauty of your poetry.

And lastly, this book would not be possible without blessings from the Source of All, the spirit who moves through each of us as we're guided on our journeys.

One

LOVE

HUNDREDS OF WAYS

Let the beauty we love be what we do.
There are hundreds of ways to kneel and kiss
      the ground.

RUMI
(1207—1273)
TRANSLATED BY COLEMAN BARKS

UNENDING LOVE

We are loved
by an unending love.
We are embraced
by arms that find us
even when
we are hidden from ourselves.
We are touched
by fingers that soothe us
even when
we are too proud for soothing.
We are counseled
by voices that guide us
even when
we are too embittered to hear.
We are loved
by an unending love.
We are supported
by hands that uplift us
even in
the midst of a fall.

Love

We are urged on
by eyes that meet us
even when
wc are too weak for meeting.
We are loved
by an unending love.
Embraced, touched, soothed, and counseled . . .
ours are the arms,
the fingers, the voices;
ours are the hands,
the eyes, the smiles;
We are loved
by an unending love.

RABBI RAMI M. SHAPIRO

ONE AT A TIME

Maybe we make it too hard,
this dream of perfect community.
I say
love the one.
Love the one neighbor well.
Look out over the railroad tracks
where the wasted and broken souls
shuffle, always alone, through the snow,
and then come home to the face of your friend,
to those whose deepest wish is for you to be, at last,
nothing but yourself,
and give thanks, one friend at a time,
one neighbor at a time
while we grow,
flower by flower,
into the garden of God.

GEORGE PERREAULT

Simply Being Loved

So I began to stop and think when somebody entered the room: If I loved this person, how would I behave toward him or her? And, of course, what I found was that the more I acted this way, the more loving and sensitive I became. And the other people are changed by simply being loved; it really becomes easier to love them. With this basic approach, over time I changed myself, my body, my state of health, my relationships, and many other aspects of my life.

BERNIE SIEGEL

To Love and Be Loved

None of us has the power
to make someone else love us.
But we all have the power to give away love,
to love other people. And if we do so,
we change the kind of person we are,
and we change the kind of world we live in.

RABBI HAROLD KUSHNER

THE GOLDEN ARROW

It lasts only a short time, this body;
time itself is nothing but imagination.

Love is the truth that cuts through all the dimensions,
an arrow flickering gold.

Love is the river that flows from one heart to the next
on its way to the ocean.

Love is the whole landscape
in every light.

Love is the voice, the gaze, the kiss of beings
practicing to be gods.

JANINE CANAN

DID I FILL MY LIFE WITH LOVE?

In the end, I think my greatest concerns will be,
How much love did I have in my life?
How did I share my love? Who loved me?
Whom did I treasure?
Whose lives did I impact?
Did my life make a difference to someone else?
How did I serve the world?
I'm certain that my only concerns will be about
How I did or did not fill my life with love.

RICHARD CARLSON

. . . .

PEACE

Begin with Children

If we are to teach real peace in this world and if we are to carry on a real war against war, we shall have to begin with children; and if they will grow up in their natural innocence, we won't have to struggle; we won't have to pass fruitless, idle resolutions, but we shall go from love to love and peace to peace, until at last all the corners of the world are covered with that peace and love for which, consciously or unconsciously, the whole world is hungering.

MAHATMA MOHANDAS GANDHI
INDIA, NOVEMBER 19, 1931

PEACE

Peace
is not
the absence of conflict,
but
the handling of conflict
without
loss of balance.

RABBI RAMI M. SHAPIRO

The Saint Francis Prayer

Lord, make me an instrument of your peace;
Where there is hatred, let me sow love;
Where there is injury, pardon;
Where there is discord, union;
Where there is doubt, faith;
Where there is despair, hope;
Where there is sadness, joy;
Where there is darkness, light.

O Divine Master,
Grant that I may not so much seek to be consoled
    as to console.
Not so much to be understood as to understand.
Not so much to be loved as to love.
For it is in giving that we receive,
In pardoning that we are pardoned,
And in dying that we are born to eternal life.

SAINT FRANCIS OF ASSISI
(1181–1226)

Peace

So Must Peace Come

Human felicity is produced not so much by
great pieces of good fortune that seldom happen,
as by little advantages that occur every day.

BENJAMIN FRANKLIN

So must peace come,
not by the momentous
stroke of pen on paper—
a peace treaty,
an arms limitation,
a nuclear freeze—
but slowly, silently,
from every inner heart
whose prayer for peace
is a nugget of gold
dropped into the center
of the world's desire.
The ripples move
into wider and ever wider

circles until one day
they will have reached
around the earth and come
again to their beginning.
Then peace will cover
the earth and the seas
and reach into the farthest
eternities of space.

So must peace come
from the heart of everyone.

ELIZABETH SEARLE LAMB

A Child's Prayer for Peace

Hello God,
Can you hear me
above all the noise?
It's us fighting one another.
Please help us to stop all our wars.
Amen

JOSEPHINE DAVIES
AGE 9

THE WORK OF PEACE

Give us courage, O Lord, to stand up and be counted,
to stand up for those who cannot stand up for themselves,
to stand up for ourselves when it is needful for us to do so.
Let us fear nothing more than we fear you.
Let us love nothing more than we love you,
for thus we shall fear nothing also . . .
Let us seek no other peace but the peace which is yours,
and make us its instruments,
opening our eyes and our ears and our hearts,
so that we should know always what work of peace
we may do for you.

ALAN PATON
(1903–1988)

LOVE ONE ANOTHER

God, one of my teachers told us in class that in some
countries white people don't like black people.
But the Bible says that you made everybody in the
world. So please try and make people stop hating
one another and love one another instead. I believe
that will stop all the wars and bring peace.

A CHILD'S PRAYER FROM LIBERIA

How to End War?

Dear God

We cannot merely pray to You to end war;
For we know that You have made the world in a way
That we must find our own paths to peace
Within ourselves and with our neighbors.
We cannot merely pray to You to end starvation;
For You have already given us the resources
With which to feed the entire world
If we would only use them wisely.
We cannot merely pray to You
To root out prejudice,
For You have already given us eyes
With which to see the good in all,
If we would only use them rightly.
We cannot merely pray to You to end despair,
For You have already given us the power
To clear away slums and to give hope
If we would only use our power justly.

We cannot merely pray to You to end disease,
For You have already given us great minds with which
To search out cures and healing,
If we would only use them constructively.
Therefore we pray to You instead
For strength, determination, and willpower,
To do instead of just to pray,
To become instead of merely to wish.

JACK RIEMER

THE MEETING

Out beyond ideas
of wrongdoing and rightdoing,
there is a field.
I'll meet you there.

RUMI
(1207—1273)
TRANSLATED BY COLEMAN BARKS

....
Peace

The Body Politic of Peace

Listen.
The body is not
a battleground,
as some people
would like you
to believe.
The body knows
peace; peace, after
all, is the body's
natural state.
Think of the body
in repose, the way
muscles loosen,
breath opens up;
think of the body
in love. It knows
what to do. It is
our mind that does
not. It is our mind
that makes us feel
separate, isolated,

it is our mind that
dreams up war.
The body says no,
come back to me,
I am fragile and strong
and I connect you
to your brothers and sisters.
I connect you to the earth.
Come back to the heartbeat,
the pulse, the rhythm
we all walk to, regardless
of nation or color. Come back
to the breath—inhale, take the world
deep into your lungs; exhale,
give yourself back fully.
This is what the body says:
release the peace
that lives within your skin.

GAYLE BRANDEIS

Peace

If There Is Light in the Soul

If there is light in the soul,
There will be beauty in the person.
If there is beauty in the person,
There will be harmony in the home.
If there is harmony in the home,
There will be order in the nation.
If there is order in the nation,
There will be peace in the world.

CHINESE PROVERB

. . . .

Three

FORGIVENESS

When We Remember Our Enemies

What heart has not acknowledged the influence of
this hour, the sweet and soothing hour of twilight—
the hour of love—the hour of adoration—the
hour of rest—when we think of those we love
only to regret that we have not loved them more
dearly; when we remember our enemies only to
forgive them.

HENRY WADSWORTH LONGFELLOW
(1807–1882)

SABBATH OF FORGIVENESS

Tonight is a Sabbath of Forgiveness,
a night devoted to healing and repair.
What hurts us this night?
What troubles and haunts us?
What have we done this past year
that we wish we had not done?
What have we felt this past year
that we wish we had not felt?
What has happened to us that caused us pain?
What pain have we caused others?
We cannot undo what has been done.
We cannot unfeel what has been felt.
We cannot pretend to not hurting
unless we pretend to not caring.
But we do care.

Forgiveness

And because we care—
for ourselves and for others—
because we care,
we hurt.
Living includes hurting.
But it also includes healing.
Living includes making mistakes.
But it also includes correcting them.
It is not enough to be sorry;
it is only enough when we do rightly the next time.

RABBI RAMI M. SHAPIRO

Forgiveness

I Was Wrong—Forgive Me

Lord,
help me to face the truth about myself.
Help me to hear my words as others hear them,
to see my face as others see me;
let me be honest enough to recognize my
    impatience and conceit;
let me recognize my anger and selfishness;
give me sufficient humility to accept my own
    weaknesses
for what they are.
Give me the grace—at least in your presence—
to say, "I was wrong—forgive me."

FRANK TOPPING

THE JOY OF COMING UNSTUCK

Of all the unfairness in life, O God, forgiveness seems the most unfair. It feels like we lose twice: first the trouble then having to give up our anger.

Ease our confusion.

Help us understand that expressing righteous anger and seeking justice is not the same as "getting even." And, really, what's "fair" about staying stuck like gum on a shoe to a past hurt? "Fair" is becoming unstuck. Nudge us when we're tempted to stay stuck in the "miserable fairness of not forgiving." When we forgive, we set someone free, but not who we suspected: the captive is us.

MARGARET ANNE HUFFMAN

Four

COMPASSION

REVERENCE FOR LIFE

May I follow a life of compassion in pity for
the suffering of all living things. Teach me to live
with reverence for life everywhere, to treat life as
sacred, and respect all that breathes. O Father,
I grope amid the shadows of doubt and fear, but I
long to advance toward the light. Help me to fling
my life like a flaming firebrand into the gathering
darkness of the world.

ATTRIBUTED TO ALBERT SCHWEITZER
(1875–1965)

THE TRUE MEANING OF COMPASSION

We are capable of suffering with our world,
and that is the true meaning of compassion.
It enables us to recognize our profound interconnectedness
with all beings . . .
It is a measure of your humanity
and your maturity.
It is a measure of your open heart,
and as your heart breaks open
there will be room for the world to heal.

JOANNA MACY

GIVE ME SOMEONE

Lord,
when I am famished,
    give me someone who needs food;
when I am thirsty,
    send me someone who needs water;
when I am cold,
    send me someone to warm;
when I am hurting,
    send me someone to console;
when my cross becomes heavy,
    give me another's cross to share;
when I am poor,
    lead someone needy to me;
when I have no time,
    give me someone to help for a moment;
when I am humiliated,
    give me someone to praise;
when I am discouraged,
    send me someone to encourage;

when I need another's understanding,
    give me someone who needs mine;
when I need somebody to take care of me,
    send me someone to care for;
when I think of myself,
    turn my thoughts toward another.

AUTHOR UNKNOWN
JAPAN, TWENTIETH CENTURY
(TRANSLATED BY MARY-THERESA MCCARTHY)

Caught on the Barb

How often, God of Compassion, we criticize and turn away from weird or disturbing behavior of others, not knowing that they, like a fish on a line, have been caught on one of life's hooks. Remind us to look beneath the surface before we condemn and reject. Send us to lend a helping, unhooking hand.

MARGARET ANNE HUFFMAN

SEND US OUT

Lord of the Universe
look in love upon your people.
Pour the healing oil of your compassion
on a world that is wounded and dying.
Send us out in search of the lost,
to comfort the afflicted,
to bind up the broken,
And to free those trapped
under the rubble of their fallen dreams.

SHEILA CASSIDY

The Essence of Compassion

The whole idea of compassion is based on a keen awareness of the interdependence of all these living beings, which are all part of one another and all involved in one another.

THOMAS MERTON
(1915–1968)

WAKING UP

Waking up this morning, I smile.
Twenty-four brand new hours are before me.
I vow to live fully in each moment
and to look at all beings
with eyes of compassion.

THICH NHAT HANH

Litany

Gather up
In the arms of your pity
The sick, the depraved,
The desperate, the tired,
All the scum
Of our weary city
Gather up
In the arms of your pity.
Gather up
In the arms of your love—
Those who expect
No love from above.

LANGSTON HUGHES
(1902—1967)

THE SUN

Like the sun's rays
compassion travels great distances.
We are warmed and fed by its presence.
Lord, help us illuminate our world
with an act of kindness
towards someone in need today.

SHIRLEY KOBAR

Prayer for a World Vision

Help us to live together as people who have
    been forgiven a great debt.
Help us to be gentle, walking softly with one another.
Help us to be understanding, lest we shall add
    to the world's sorrow or cause to flow one
    needless tear.
Help us to stand for what is right, not because it
    may yield dividends later, but because it is
    right now.
Help us to be as anxious that the rights of
    others shall be recognized as we are that our
    own shall be established.
Help us to be as eager to forgive others as we are
    to seek forgiveness.
Help us to know no barriers of creed or race,
    that our love may be like Thine.
God, help us all to be ministers of mercy and
    ambassadors of kindness.   Amen.

PETER MARSHALL

LORD, OPEN OUR EYES

Lord, open our eyes,
That we may see you in our brothers and sisters.
Lord, open our ears,
That we may hear the cries of the hungry, the cold,
the frightened, the oppressed.
Lord, open our hearts,
That we may love each other as you love us.
Renew in us your spirit
Lord, free us and make us one.

MOTHER TERESA
(1910–1997)

....

Five

SPIRITUALITY

SERENITY

Do not be in a hurry
to fill up an empty space
with words and embellishments,
before it has been filled
with a deep interior peace.

FATHER ALEXANDER ELCHANINOV

What We Can Do

Live cleanly, simply:
one chair for each of us, one for a guest;
beans every shade of earth in clear glass jars;
our windows turned to face the rising sun.

Treasure the beauty human hands have made:
worn-spined books piled high on a pine shelf;
a bowl glazed the colors of grass and water;
a child's red-painted rocker at the hearth.

Walk gently on the earth:
a house stained the color of trees, a leaf-green roof;
a fruit tree planted for each child we bear;
a prayer of thanks for every seed.

REBECCA BAGGETT

Spirituality

PRAYER TO MOTHER EARTH

Every step that we take upon you
should be done in a sacred manner;
each step should be
as a prayer.

BLACK ELK

On Paths that Have Heart

For me there is only the traveling
on paths that have heart,
on any path that may have heart.
There I travel,
and the only worthwhile challenge
is to traverse its full length.
And there I travel,
looking, looking,
breathlessly.

CARLOS CASTAÑEDA
(1931–1998)

LETTING GO

Let go of the place that holds,
let go of the place that flinches,
let go of the place that controls,
let go of the place that fears.
Just let the ground support me. . . .
Walking in the dark night
is a way to practice faith,
a way to build confidence
in the unknown. . . .
I learn to practice courage in
the vastness of what I can't see. . . .

STEPHANIE KAZA

DISTINCTION

Darkness and light,
twins of a single mother birthing
all and nothingness with each breath.
We cannot know one while ignoring the other;
we cannot trust one while distrusting the other;
we cannot embrace one while fleeing the other;
we are the one, we are the other.

Light and dark, in and out, up and down—
each known only from the other.
Male and female, good and evil, right and wrong—
each incomprehensible without the other.

RABBI RAMI M. SHAPIRO

PLEASE PRINT LEGIBLY

I dislike discussion of the godhead
and shun all speculation as to its gender
denomination or intent

But in the space provided on forms
and application blanks, "What is your
religious preference?" I always answer

"Yes."

MEREDITH SABINI

WINDCHIMES

On my porch I am
embracing the sun—

These windchimes are
subdued bells of a distant
church;

These bees
genuflect
on rows of potted marigolds—

The breeze pushes through trees.

Birds leave their branches;
journey; dip; drink;
wash in ritual ablution.

I meditate:

I ask the creator of that searing sun
to energize me;

I ask that the sound of my life
echo
ethereal as windchimes,
harmonious as the song
echoing from the church
beyond—

I ask that I will be cleansed
and refreshed and empowered—
a pilgrim of the earth;

I ask that I find
the elusive nectar
in a cache both as hidden and obvious
as the sweetness
in the dependable marigold.

DONNA WAHLERT

THE ONLY PRAYER

If the only prayer you say in your entire life is
"Thank you," that would suffice.

MEISTER ECKHART

The Guest House

This being human is a guest house.
Every morning a new arrival.

A joy, a depression, a meanness,
some momentary awareness comes
as an unexpected visitor.

Welcome and entertain them all!
Even if they're a crowd of sorrows,
who violently sweep your house
empty of its furniture,
still, treat each guest honorably.
He may be clearing you out
for some new delight.

The dark thought, the shame, the malice,
meet them at the door laughing,
and invite them in.

Be grateful for whoever comes,
because each has been sent
as a guide from beyond.

RUMI
(1207–1273)
TRANSLATED BY COLEMAN BARKS

I Sought My Soul

I sought my soul,
but my soul I could not see,
I sought my God,
but my God eluded me,
I sought my brother
and found all three.

AUTHOR UNKNOWN

The Blessing of Failures

O God, teach us to know that failure is as much
a part of life as success—and whether it shall
be evil or good depends upon the way we meet it—
if we face it listlessly and daunted, angrily
or vengefully, then indeed is it evil for it
spells death. But if we let our failures stand as
guideposts and as warnings—as beacons and as
guardians—then is honest failure far better than
stolen success, and but a part of that great training
which God gives us to make us men and women.
The race is not to the swift—nor the battle to the
strong, O God.   Amen.

W. E. B. DUBOIS
(1868–1963)

63
....
Spirituality

On All Steps as Steps on the Way

When there is nowhere
    that you have determined
        to call your own,
then no matter where you go
    you are always going home.

BUDDHIST PROVERB
(TRANSLATED BY STEVEN D. CARTER)

Remembrance

I sit on this wind-swept cliff
and stare at the sea and surf,
dazzling blue and white.

I think of times long gone,
of those who sat here
and stared at these same waters.
I wonder—is this what they saw?
Is this what they meant by Spirit?
This screaming fury of waves
pounding the sand,
of wind streaming the heights,
sun gleaming on the waves?
The relentless power of nature
that will not be controlled?

Yes, I believe this is what they saw.
This is their world.
The world of the Spirit.

LUKAS JAI CLARY
AGE 15

Whatever Comes

You have to accept
whatever comes and the
only important thing is
that you meet it with
courage and with the best
that you have to give.

ELEANOR ROOSEVELT
(1884–1962)

Yield and Overcome

Yield and overcome;
Bend and be straight;
Empty and be full;
Wear out and be new;
Have little and gain;
Have much and be confused.

Therefore wise souls embrace the one
And set an example to all.
Not putting on a display,
They shine forth.
Not justifying themselves,
They are distinguished.
Not boasting,
They receive recognition.
Not bragging,
They never falter.
They do not quarrel,

So no one quarrels with them.
Therefore the ancients say,
     "Yield and overcome."
Is that an empty saying?
Be really whole,
And all things will come to you.

LAO-TZU

BLESSINGS OF THE HEART

If you are poor,
live wisely.
If you have riches,
live wisely.
It is not your station in life
but your heart
that brings blessings.

THE BUDDHA

THE WATERCOURSE WAY

The highest good is like water,
For the good of water is that
it nourishes everything without striving.

The most gentle thing in the world
overrides the most hard.

How do coves and oceans become kings
of a hundred rivers?
Because they are good at keeping low—

That is how they are kings
of the hundred rivers.

Nothing in the world is weaker than water,
But it has no better in overcoming the hard.

LAO-TZU

A GREAT SECRET

I shall tell you a great secret, my friend.
Do not wait for the last judgment;
it takes place every day.

ALBERT CAMUS
(1913–1960)

Six

NATURE
AND THE
ENVIRONMENT

LOST

Stand still. The trees ahead and the bushes beside you
Are not Lost. Wherever you are is called Here,
And you must treat it as a powerful stranger,
Must ask permission to know it and be known.
The forest breathes. Listen. It answers,
I have made this place around you.
If you leave it, you may come back again, saying Here.
No two branches are the same to Raven.
No two trees are the same to Wren.
If what a tree or a bush does is lost on you,
You are surely lost. Stand still. The forest knows
Where you are. You must let it find you.

DAVID WAGONER

*Nature and the
Environment*

SLEEPING IN THE FOREST

I thought the earth
remembered me, she
took me back so tenderly, arranging
her dark skirts, her pockets
full of lichens and seeds. I slept
as never before, a stone
on the riverbed, nothing
between me and the white fire of the stars
but my thoughts, and they floated
light as moths among the branches
of the perfect trees. All night
I heard the small kingdoms breathing
around me, the insects, and the birds
who do their work in the darkness. All night
I rose and fell, as if in water, grappling
with a luminous doom. By morning
I had vanished at least a dozen times
into something better.

MARY OLIVER

*Nature and the
Environment*

SAINTS

The pale flowers of the dogwood
outside this window are saints.
The little yellow flowers that nobody notices
on the edge of that road are saints
looking up into the face of God.

This leaf has its own texture
and its own pattern of veins
and its own holy shape,
and the bass and trout hiding in the deep pools
of the river are canonized
by their beauty and their strength.

The lakes hidden among the hills are saints,
and the sea too is a saint who praises God
without interruption in her majestic dance.

THOMAS MERTON
(1915–1968)

WIND SONG

I am the wind of many names
With boundless tales to tell.
I grace the clouds of Heaven's realm
And fan the fires of Hell.

I am the breeze of ancient seas
Before life crawled ashore;
I watched the rise and fall of beast
So many times before.

I am the primal wail of time
That weathers men and stone.
I've danced the sanctity of space
Where angel wings have flown.

I am the restless storm of change,
The gentle breath of dawn;
I've howled from time eternal
And I'll blow when you are gone.

I am the wind of war and peace
That honors right nor wrong.
I am the mystic voice of God—
Come listen to my song.

C. DAVID HAY

Nature and the
Environment

On Guardian Angels

Perhaps my angels have all along been birds.
How often am I out of their sight?
Even when I'm indoors, they come
to the window, seek me, keep watch.

So what if I can't understand their speech?
As long as the dawn hears the rooster and the waves
take their cue from the gulls, I too can have
their music without demanding sense of it.

In the main, my angels are small, brown sparrows,
who fly like tiny grapeshot & fastidiously watch,
but call little attention to themselves. They even seem
indifferent; but isn't that a perfect disguise?

RICHARD BEBAN

*Nature and the
Environment*

TREES

I think that I shall never see
A poem lovely as a tree.

A tree whose hungry mouth is pressed
Against the earth's sweet flowing breast;

A tree that looks at God all day
And lifts her leafy arms to pray;

A tree that may in summer wear
A nest of robins in her hair;

Upon whose bosom snow has lain;
Who intimately lives with rain.

Poems are made by fools like me,
But only God can make a tree.

JOYCE KILMER

Praise to the Earth

About the trees my arms I wound
Like one gone mad, I hugged the ground
I raised my quivering arms up high
I laughed and laughed into the sky.

AUTHOR UNKNOWN

NAVAJO CHANT

The mountains, I become part of it . . .
The herbs, the fir tree, I become part of it.
The morning mists, the clouds, the gathering
    waters,
I become part of it.
The wilderness, the dewdrops, the
        pollen . . .
I become part of it.

AUTHOR UNKNOWN

IF LOVE TAKES SHAPE

A white egret
flies up suddenly
from the small pond
round in the cut field.
My steps on the road
have startled it; I am not
expected here. Its wings spread wide,
its neck lies long: a strong
and timid spirit.
I know it as a message
rising high into the sky,
water and earth have sent it.

VIRGINIA BARRETT

To Think Like a Planet

To survive
our minds must taste redwood
and agate, octopi,
bat, and in the bat's mouth,
insect. It's hard
to think like a planet.
We've got to try.

JAMES BERTOLINO

*Nature and the
Environment*

SYLVAN

The quietude of the forest,
like a grand cathedral,
welcomes me.
Every leaf is divinity,
every tree holds
a moment of eternity.

CORRINE DE WINTER

FORESTRY

There has never been ritual
enough for the dying of trees
nothing to validate the deep
sense of loss that will soon
rise up in us like March
maple sap, the privation
in our surroundings that
disorients daily. We should
dance and chant around them
reciting verses of worshipful
praise to the elements that
have raised rain to scented
pitch, ring after ring of seasons,
or, at least, before starting
the chain saw, look up in awe
at what stands stapling heaven
to the earth, and will soon be
nothing but a large, silent hole
in the sky
as in the ground.

MAUREEN TOLMAN FLANNERY

WILD STRAWBERRIES

a field without tar
or power lines
or groundhog killers

a field quiet
as fallen pine needles—
loud as an angry bluejay

a field where poems grow
like wild strawberries

RALPH S. COLEMAN

NATURAL THEOLOGY

You read it in the blue wind,
the blue water, the rock spill,
the blue hill

rising like a phoenix from ash. Some mind
makes itself known through the markings of light
on air; where earth rolls, right

comes after, our planet's bright spoor. . . . If you
        look, you'll find
truth etched on the tree trunk,
the shark's tooth, a shell, a hunk

of root and soil. Study from beginning to end.
Alpha and omega—these are the cirrus alphabet,
the Gnostics' cloudy "so—and yet."

If a tree falls in a forest, a scared hind
leaps, hearing branches break;
you crawl under the log and shake

honey out of a hollow, eggs from a nest, ants from
    the end
of a stick; resting, you read God's name on the back
    of a bass
in a blue pool; God grows everywhere, like grass.

KELLY CHERRY

Nature and the
Environment

We Are a Part of the Earth

... the earth's swift rivers,
the silent footsteps of
spring, the sparkling
ripples on the surface of
the ponds, the bright
colors of the birds. We
are a part of the earth and
it is a part of us.

CHIEF SEATTLE
(1786–1866)

*Nature and the
Environment*

AFFAIR IN THE GARDEN

Beneath the overgrown grass swells the rich brown body
of the Earth. I want to throw myself down on it,
embrace it. I want to hug the trees, their high
summer lushness a green temptation.
Wildflowers appear, planted years ago,
flirtatiously blooming now as if they had
all the time in the world to grow
so beautiful and, of course, they do.
This is why as I bask in August sun
in the garden with perfumed breeze
stroking my bare legs and arms and face,
I am totally in love, wanting only to be
one with this pulsing planet.

ARLENE GAY LEVINE

ODE TO THE RAIN

Glistening fingers caress the earth
giving birth to what nourishes me, sparrow, tree
Oh, rain! You are much maligned
Unkind people casually curse
the generosity of your silver kiss

Your gifts wrapped in the guise of inconvenience
fall gently on us all
We who insist on sun
and forget when your work is done
we are restored

Clean our sullied spirits,
the refuse of our parched hearts
Play the symphony of your sweet drops
upon the deserts we've created of our lives
so the seed of one kind deed can sprout
fragile and full of hope in us all

ARLENE GAY LEVINE

RIVER

Slowly grinding sandstone,
layers of shale and limestone
that have known other waters,
this river has worn its way
down to black plutonic rock,
once molten magma
fused deep in the Earth.

Those who see river spirits
tell us that these waters
know what they are; know
that their job is to carve
canyons, dark mouths telling
endless stories of silt;

and to move these mountains
piece by piece, teaching
that all of life is simply
letting go.

PENNY HARTER

*Nature and the
Environment*

SIMPLY PUT

—spider, gnat, house-fly, horse-fly,
silverfish, cricket, caterpillar, ladybug,
ant, bee, pill bug, earthworm,

rabbit!

—dandelion, forget-me-not, buttercup,
daffodil, lily, rose, lilac, tulip,
azalea, hyacinth, lily
of the valley, many birds.

I believe
in God.

MARYLISA W. DEDOMENICIS

*Nature and the
Environment*

THE PEACE OF WILD THINGS

When despair for the world grows in me
and I wake in the night at the least sound
in fear of what my life and my children's lives
    may be,
I go and lie down where the wood drake
rests in his beauty on the water, and the great
    heron feeds,
I come into the peace of wild things
who do not tax their lives with forethought
of grief. I come into the presence of still water.
And I feel above me the day-blind stars
waiting with their light. For a time
I rest in the grace of the world, and am free.

WENDELL BERRY

Nature and the
Environment

I MAKE MY HOME IN THE MOUNTAINS

You ask why I live,
alone in the mountain forest,

and I smile and am silent
until even my soul grows quiet.

The peach trees blossom.
The water continues to flow.

I live in the other world,
one that lies beyond the human.

LI PO
(701–762)
TRANSLATED FROM THE CHINESE BY SAM HAMILL

*Nature and the
Environment*

. . . .

Seven

CHILDREN

WHATEVER SHE INVITES

Out in the forest where we roam,
my daughter takes me by the hand
and with a surety she found there
shows me where to turn:
"Look at the trees! Look up!
Be careful, papa!"

I am a child
in her confidence. I am
whatever she invites.
Wonder full
is our world.

RICK KEMPA

A SENSE OF WONDER

If I had influence with the good fairy
who is supposed to preside over
the christening of all children
I should ask that her gift to each child in the world
be a sense of wonder so
indestructible that it would last
throughout life,
as an unfailing antidote against
the boredom and disenchantments of later years,
the sterile preoccupation with
things that are artificial,
the alienation from the sources of our strength.

RACHEL CARSON
(1907–1964)

TEACH YOUR CHILDREN

Teach your children
what we have taught our children—
that the earth is our mother.
Whatever befalls the earth
befalls the sons and daughters of the earth.

We did not weave the web of life,
We are merely a strand in it.
Whatever we do to the web,
we do to ourselves. . . .

CHIEF SEATTLE
(1786–1866)

STAR CONVERSATIONS

Arc to Arcturus,

—that's what she remembered—
and *speed to Spica.*
He had taught her to identify
all the summer constellations,
and the day after Independence Day
she had seen Jupiter and its four moons—
of course, there had been others in the astronomy class,
but she remembered it all in a special way,
as if the instruction had been molded to her needs—

                         he was the one who believed in her.

The day of the Star Party was also fresh in her mind.
All the kids in her class had come, some with
     their parents,
and the boys who were playing basketball had lingered
to peer through the telescope
long after Corvus appeared near the horizon.

Now she had come back to the school to see him,
to tell him that she was working as an astrophysicist,
working with gas chromatographs and spectrographs,

instruments, the very mention of whose names,
would bring sparkle to his eyes;

                    to tell him she had made it.
But he was not there.

"He left a long while back," a lady at the office said,
"Went to the Philippines, if I remember correctly."
"I was his student," the young woman said,
but in the busy office activity she had interrupted
her words dissipated without acknowledgment.

As she walked away from school
she felt warm with wonder of the world;
she also felt a sadness that was in all things.

That night she walked outside her house
and looked at the sky:
the constellations were shifting patterns, forming
    new shapes,
and an old familiar voice in a new place was telling
    children stories about the stars.

S. RAMNATH

Children

LITTLE LIVES

It is not enough
to tell a child how to behave,
or how to find happiness.
Words are plentiful.
Little lives are fragile.
We must show them in every gesture
how to build a meaningful life,
how to extend our kindness to others
and forgive cruelty by doing so.
We must show them
how something as easy as a smile
can hold the power to heal.

CORRINE DE WINTER

Children

THE POTENTIALITY OF THE HUMAN RACE

In every child who is born,
under no matter what circumstances,
and of no matter what parents, the
potentiality of the human race
is born again . . .

JAMES AGEE

The Child's Sob

But the child's sob in the silence curses deeper than
the strong man in his wrath.

ELIZABETH BARRETT BROWNING
(1806–1861)

ADVICE

I wonder even as I know
If it is still the same,
That children dream of being great,
And knowing wealth and fame.
I think of telling them sometimes
Of things with worth that are real,
Of how success is many things
Such as a peace we feel.
But as I do, I know no good
Will come of my advice,
For lessons must be learned, you know,
By stumbling once or twice.
Mere words can never take the place
Of lessons children see;
It's with their eyes and hearts they learn
Of life's reality.

HILDA SANDERSON

A FRESH DREAM

I track the messages
my baby sends
rippling through my being.

I see her,
already in my arms
nuzzling, elegant
like the surge of a fresh dream
filled with emerald mist
of uncharted horizons.

I visualize her at ten,
on a journey
through twisted dollops
of amber rocks,
smelling petals with the feel of satin,
studying the wonder
of a far away day moon.

My prayers are a tangle
of hopes and entreaty
that my daughter will find her new world
filled with deeds of compassion
where she can make herself
at home in the universe.

BLANCHE ROSLOFF

CHALLENGE TO THE CHILD

Explore the earth as you now find it.
Solve new mysteries; find the stone.
Crawl to where the sphere turns firmament.
Isolate to know for certain you are not alone.
Touch the wedding of the waters:
See the elements combine.
Read the wordless book of nature
Where the spirit's clearly writ.
Make the modern magic thine.
Go, my child, into the world.
Find yourself in knowing it.

MAUREEN TOLMAN FLANNERY

Children

Eight

FRIENDS

AND

FAMILY

FRIENDSHIP

Oh, the comfort—the inexpressible comfort
   of feeling safe with a person,
Having neither to weigh thoughts,
Nor measure words—but pouring them
All right out—just as they are—
Chaff and grain together—
Certain that a faithful hand will
Take and sift them—
Keep what is worth keeping—
And with the breath of kindness
Blow the rest away.

DINAH MARIA MULOCK CRAIK

NEW FRIENDS AND OLD FRIENDS

Make new friends, but keep the old;
Those are silver, these are gold.
New-made friendships, like new wine,
Age will mellow and refine.
Friendships that have stood the test—
Time and change—are surely best;
Brow may wrinkle, hair grow gray;
Friendship never knows decay.
For 'mid old friends, tried and true,
Once more we our youth renew.
But old friends, alas! may die;
New friends must their place supply.
Cherish friendship in your breast—
New is good, but old is best;
Make new friends, but keep the old;
Those are silver, these are gold.

JOSEPH PARRY

*Friends and
Family*

THE FRIEND WHO JUST STANDS BY

When trouble comes your soul to try,
You love the friend who just "stands by."
Perhaps there's nothing he can do—
The thing is strictly up to you;
For there are troubles all your own,
And paths the soul must tread alone;
Times when love cannot smooth the road
Nor friendship lift the heavy load,
But just to know you have a friend
Who will "stand by" until the end,
Whose sympathy through all endures,
Whose warm handclasp is always yours—
It helps, some way, to pull you through,
Although there's nothing he can do.
And so with fervent heart you cry,
"God bless the friend who just 'stands by'!"

B. Y. WILLIAMS
(1876–1951)

KICKING AND SCREAMING
INTO THE CLASSROOM

I believe that we invite
people into our lives,
especially our partners,
to be our teachers.
The irony of this is that,
having invited them to be our teachers,
we then go kicking and screaming
into the classroom!

PATRICIA LOVE

*Friends and
Family*

THE FAMILY CIRCLE

Dear God, from whom every family
  receives its true name,
I pray for all the members of my family:
for those who are growing up,
that they may increase in wisdom and love;
for those facing changes,
that they may meet them with hope;
for those who are weak,
that they may find strength;
for those with heavy burdens,
that they may carry them lightly;
for those who are old and frail,
that they may grow in faith.

AUTHOR UNKNOWN

*Friends and
Family*

LOOK WITHIN

It isn't necessary to go
out to the slums
to find poverty
and a lack of love.
There is someone who
suffers in every
family.

MOTHER TERESA
(1910–1997)

*Friends and
Family*

A GAELIC BLESSING

May the road rise to meet you,
May the wind be always at your back,
May the sun shine warm on your face,
The rain fall softly on your fields,
And until we meet again
May God hold you in the palm of his hand.

AUTHOR UNKNOWN

Nine

COMMUNITY
AND WORLDLY
CONCERNS

Somewhere in a Small Village

Somewhere in a small village
on the edge of the world,
or in a crowded city
or on an island as complex as Sicily,
a man or a woman or a child
has a life so foreign from mine,

it is as different as sky from earth, yet it is the same.

Knowing only the home place,
family,
and sometimes little more than the essentials for
    surviving,
sometimes as rich as a king, yet it is the same.

It is a life as full
and rich and meaningful as any.
And like mine,

centered on one's experience.

*Community
and Worldly
Concerns*

So, sitting on a front stoop in Palermo
or on a rocket ship to outer space,

no life is any better than any other.

No time is more important.
No birth is less significant.
No death is more lonely or personal.

Each is all
and everything
and enough

for each and every one.

RALPH SCHILLACE

SO MANY GODS, SO MANY CREEDS

So many gods, so many creeds,
So many paths that wind and wind,
When just the art of being kind
Is all this sad world needs.

AUTHOR UNKNOWN

*Community
and Worldly
Concerns*

STOPPING BY A CANDY SHELF

If only
the people of the world
could keep
their true separate flavors
and hold tight to each other
the way
Life Savers do.

IDA FASEL

*Community
and Worldly
Concerns*

This Is Our Hope

This is our hope, this is the faith that I go back South with.

With this faith we will be able to hew out of the mountain of despair a stone of hope. With this faith we will be able to transform the jangling discords of our nation into a beautiful symphony of brotherhood.

With this faith we will be able to work together, to pray together, to struggle together, to go to jail together, to stand up for freedom together, knowing that we will be free one day. . . .

MARTIN LUTHER KING JR.
(1929–1968)

MAY I BE A PROTECTOR

May I be a protector to those without protection,
A leader for those who journey,
And a boat, a bridge, a passage
For those desiring the further shore.

May the pain of every living creature
Be completely cleared away.
May I be the doctor and the medicine
And may I be the nurse
For all sick beings in the world
Until everyone is healed.

SOGYAL RINPOCHE
(TIBETAN BUDDHIST TEACHER)

*Community
and Worldly
Concerns*

The Soul Has No Color

You look at this container,
and just because
of my skin's pigmentation
you try to cram me
in a crayon box.
But the soul has no color,
no denomination,

         no prejudice,

              no pride.

MIKE W. BLOTTENBERGER

PRAYER FOR HUMANITY

I pray that we learn to love more and demand
    less—so that our love for one another will be
    our ever-present reality and consciousness.

I pray that we experience our common humanity
    and that we understand that all of us are more
    alike than different.

I pray that I realize that my life won't work well
    unless your life works well and that our lives
    on this planet are deeply intertwined.

I pray that we learn that we have one world—and
    that we no longer separate ourselves in the
    name of national boundary lines.

*Community
and Worldly
Concerns*

I pray that we learn to disagree without throwing each other out of our hearts—and not keep ourselves upset over our differences.

I pray that we learn to forgive, for our own sake— for a heart hardened with hatred is too heavy to carry.

I pray that we settle arguments in nonviolent ways—that we learn to listen to one another and truly hear, so that all arms become obsolete.

I pray that we act less impulsively—so that love and wisdom may guide our actions.

*Community
and Worldly
Concerns*

I pray that we learn to experience the beauty in
ourselves and each other—and that we feel
deep appreciation for the good things we have.

I pray that we hear the message that God is love—
so that we no longer separate ourselves in the
name of religion.

I pray that we open our hearts and learn to live
together on this globe—so that we find our
great birthright of a loving life.

KEN KEYES JR.
(1921–1995)

*Community
and Worldly
Concerns*

TOGETHER

Let's walk together
and not apart
and see what the beauty
really is.

TREVA M. WILSON
AGE 12

SPEAKING OUT

We will have to repent in this generation
not merely for the hateful words
and actions of the bad people
but for the appalling silence
of the good people.

MARTIN LUTHER KING JR.
(1929–1968)

*Community
and Worldly
Concerns*

No Man Is an Island

No man is an island, entire of itself;
every man is a piece of the continent,
    a part of the main;
. . . any man's death diminishes me, because
I am involved in mankind;
and therefore never send to know for whom the
bell tolls; it tolls for thee.

JOHN DONNE
(1572—1631)

*Community
and Worldly
Concerns*

WHO ARE MY PEOPLE?

My people? Who are they?
I went into the church where the congregation
Worshipped my God. Were they my people?
I felt no kinship to them as they knelt there.
My people! Where are they?
I went into the land where I was born,
Where men spoke my language . . .
I was a stranger there.
"My people," my soul cried. "Who are my people?"

Last night in the rain I met an old man
Who spoke a language I do not speak,
Which marked him as one who does not know my God.
With apologetic smile he offered me
The shelter of his patched umbrella.
I met his eyes . . . and then I knew. . . .

ROSA ZAGNONI MARINONI

*Community
and Worldly
Concerns*

HOMELESS

He watches as they hurry by,
    Not giving him a glance—
They think he wants a hand-out, but
    He simply wants a chance . . .

To rise above the circumstances
    That put him where he is—
He wants the chance to try again
    To make the future his.

He needs to know someone cares
    If he should live or die,
But no compassion does he see . . .
    And he begins to cry.

He turns away and crouches down
    So no one sees his tears:
He thinks about the days ahead,
    And all the empty years.

*Community
and Worldly
Concerns*

Then suddenly, he feels a touch
    and turns his eyes above
to see a stranger standing there . . .
    Whose eyes are filled with love.

The stranger pulls him to his feet
    —His touch felt somehow odd—
And then he knew that through this man . . .
    He grasped the hand of God.

DENISE A. DEWALD

*Community
and Worldly
Concerns*

IF YOU HAVE A PARTICULAR FAITH

If you have a particular faith or religion,
that is good.
But you can survive without it
if you have love, compassion, and tolerance.
The clear proof of a person's love of God
is if that person genuinely shows
love to fellow human beings.

THE DALAI LAMA

139
. . . .
*Community
and Worldly
Concerns*

TRUE HAPPINESS

I don't know what your destiny will be,
but one thing I know:
the only ones among you
who will be truly happy
are those who will have sought
and found how to serve.

ATTRIBUTED TO ALBERT SCHWEITZER
(1875–1965)

*Community
and Worldly
Concerns*

Ten

WONDER

AND

APPRECIATION

WALKING ALONE ON A
THICKLY STARRED NIGHT

to the ringing of crickets, the bullfrog's
thrumming bass: the whole earth
is vibrating, singing.
This is a walk on the skin of things,
listening to the pulse, as the dust & swirl
of the Milky Way dance overhead,
and I walk past black trees
that are the shadows of trees,
so dark that the edge of the world
might be one step ahead,
but always the Dipper is tilting, rising over
the black cathedral of pines, always points
the way back home.

BARBARA CROOKER

ARE YOU LOOKING FOR ME?

O dear friend
in search of
My Beloved,
I wandered
All over the earth
in far and distant lands;

But on meeting
With God,
My own courtyard
Became the universe!

KABIR
(1450–1518)

*Wonder and
Appreciation*

From Joy I Came

From joy I came.
For joy I live.
And in sacred joy
I shall melt again.

YOGANANDA

SUBLIME GENEROSITY
(Excerpt)

The soul at dawn is like darkened water
that slowly begins to say *Thank you, thank you.*

Then at sunset, again, Venus gradually
changes into the moon and then the whole nightsky.

This comes of smiling back
at your smile.

The chess master says nothing,
other than moving the silent chess piece.

That I am part of the ploys
of this game makes me
amazingly happy.

RUMI
(1207—1273)
TRANSLATED BY COLEMAN BARKS

*Wonder and
Appreciation*

GOD

Just out of reach
　　　But warmly near.
Far beyond sight
　　　But sensed so clear.
Voice undefined
　　　Yet clear as song.
Never alone.
　　　A love, life long.

NANCY RUSTICI

I See Something of God Each Hour

I see something of God each hour of the twenty-
    four, and each moment then:
In the faces of men and women I see God, and in
    my own face in the glass:

I find letters from God dropped in the street, and
    every one is sign'd God's name;
And I leave them where they are, for I know that
    wheresoever I go,
Others will punctually come forever and ever.

WALT WHITMAN
(1819–1892)

ALL

Even sitting
at the kitchen table
in the frizzy heat
of an August afternoon
is a cosmic experience.
The sweet garden carrot
crunching in my mouth
becomes me.
All is spirit.

KATE ROBINSON

PRAYER

cutting open
a green pepper
dazzles

the dancing
undulation
of moist skin

tiny seeds
crowded together
into an orchestra

playing
the fragrant music
of the universe

LINDA GOODMAN ROBINER

*Wonder and
Appreciation*

MIRACLES

Why, who makes much of a miracle?
As to me I know of nothing else but miracles,
Whether I walk the streets of Manhattan . . .
Or look at strangers opposite me riding in the car,
Or watch honey-bees busy around the hive
    of a summer forenoon,
Or watch animals feeding in the fields,
Or birds, or the wonderfulness of the sundown, or
    of stars shining so quiet and bright,
Or the exquisite delicate thin curve of the new
    moon in spring . . .
To me every hour of the light and dark is a miracle,
Every cubic inch of space is a miracle,
Every square yard of the surface of the earth is
    spread with the same . . .
What stranger miracles are there?

WALT WHITMAN
(1819–1892)

*Wonder and
Appreciation*

Eleven

PRAISE

AND

CELEBRATION

A Silent Certainty

I join with the universe. I sing with
the universe. I know not my
beginning. I shall never end. Through
me move the currents of
life—attracting, repelling, creating,
decaying—I see their beauty;
I feel their power; I am overwhelmed.
Within me flow the conflicting
ambiguities of time—death in living,
pain in knowing, hope in seeking,
love in giving—I search for their
meaning; I look for their purpose;
but no one understands. Yet around me,
above me, within me lies a mystery
above all mysteries, a truth above all
truths, an assurance that fills
the earth and the starry heavens above, a
solemn knowledge, a silent certainty
that *that* which moves the universe moves me.

THOMAS L. REID

*Praise and
Celebration*

A Prayer for the Earth

Far away, we look like the marbled pupil of an eye.
This planet, full of water, is delicate as a body.
When I lie on the ground, a smell comes to me
like a field of strawberries, like my garden, and grass.

Some days I remember the beach, those days I felt
most at home, afloat in the belly of the planet, salt
and sand drifting in the green waters. The blue planet
is more than mother and more than father. We

are this planet, every bit. Daffodil, lemur, bald eagle,
all colors, sky, lake and sea, even the asphalt,
yellow school bus, quartz, mud, song, and sweet old air.
Tree blowing in the breeze, the cardinal's sharp chirp—

every night I will lie down with you, hold you
    and cherish
in my arms like a new child, you, as my dearest love.
    Amen.

LAURA LEE WASHBURN

Your Children Are We

O our Mother the Earth, O our Father the Sky,
Your children are we, and with tired backs
We bring you the gifts that you love.
Then weave for us a garment of brightness;
May the warp be the white light of morning,
May the weft be the red light of the evening,
May the fringes be the falling rain,
May the border be the standing rainbow.
Thus weave for us a garment of brightness
That we may walk fittingly where birds sing,
That we may walk fittingly where grass is green,
O our Mother the Earth, O our Father the Sky!

TEWA INDIAN
NORTH AMERICA

*Praise and
Celebration*

MAY THE LONG TIME SUN SHINE UPON YOU

May the long time sun shine upon you
all love surround you, and the pure light
within you guide you all the way on.

AUTHOR UNKNOWN

Twelve

TOLERANCE

COMBINATIONS

There is a combination for everything—
the way I wear my hair,
and you yours,
my squint
and your wide-open stare.
The combination
of words put to paper,
the combination
of words that never appear.

The Universe
combines us
and we commingle with the stars—
the way a comet passes its years
out there,
the way we pass ours
here.

JULIA OLDER

A Reflection

The moon does not mind
its distance from the sun,

nor does the sun spurn
a moon in its way,

both finding in their separateness
a space for sharing light.

MARYANNE HANNAN

Prayer of This Imperfect Me

God, let me see this world of mine
Through thankful eyes,
And see the good in even those
Whose actions I despise,
While in myself I learn to have
Simple humility,
And tolerance for all of those
Who don't agree with me.

HILDA SANDERSON

PLEA FOR TOLERANCE

If we but knew what forces helped to mold
    The lives of others from their earliest years—
    Knew something of their background, joys and tears,
And whether or not their youth was drear and cold,
Or if some dark belief had taken hold
    And kept them shackled, torn with doubts and fears
So long it crushed the force that perseveres
    And made their hearts grow prematurely old,—

Then we might judge with wiser, kindlier sight,
    And learn to put aside our pride and scorn . . .
Perhaps no one can ever quite undo
    His faults or wholly banish some past blight—
The tolerant mind is purified, reborn,
    And lifted upward to a saner view.

MARGARET E. BRUNER
(1886–1971)

GUARD ME FROM DESTRUCTIVE THOUGHTS

God, help me be warm and friendly;
        Let Your love be seen in me—
For traits I see in others,
        They may also see in me.

And guard me from destructive thoughts
        So others I don't condemn—
For when I think they're judging me . . .
        I'm really judging them.

DENISE A. DEWALD

Deliver Us from Jumping to Conclusions

Caution us, Lord, against fearing and hating all who talk and wear their hair, clothes, manners and skin color "different." How quickly we jump to conclusions, eager to distance ourselves. And, even in these cautionary days, help us spot value in all those we meet. For, O God, what opportunities we miss when we build fences to keep out "strangers" only to discover we've trapped ourselves behind a wall, too.

MARGARET ANNE HUFFMAN

Grant Me Understanding

O God, help us not to despise or oppose
what we do not understand.

WILLIAM PENN
(1644–1718)

(Expelled from Oxford University and imprisoned several
times for his Quaker faith, Penn was a passionate defender of
religious freedom. He founded the state of Pennsylvania, a
refuge for persecuted Quakers and a "holy experiment" in
religious community.)

Thirteen

HOPE
FOR THE
FUTURE

FOR A CERTAIN ARTIST

in one wide tree
he sees a boat

in milkweed seeds
the billowed sails

in ponds the sea
in stones the earth

in puddles sky
in candles stars

and in one heart
the universe

ELISAVIETTA RITCHIE

*Hope for the
Future*

HOPING

Hoping is knowing that there is love,
it is trust in tomorrow
it is falling asleep
and waking again
when the sun rises.
In the midst of a gale at sea,
it is to discover land.
In the eyes of another
it is to see that he understands you . . .
As long as there still is hope
There will also be prayer . . .
And God will be holding you
in his hands.

AUTHOR UNKNOWN

*Hope for the
Future*

TESTIMONY
(for my daughters)

I want to tell you
that the world is still beautiful.
I tell you that despite
children raped on city streets,
shot down in school rooms,
despite the slow poisons seeping
from old and hidden sins
into our air, soil, water,
despite the thinning film
that encloses our aching world.
Despite my own terror and despair.

I want you to look again and again,
to recognize the tender grasses,
curled like a baby's fine hairs
around your fingers, as a recurring
miracle, to see that the river rocks
shine like God, that the crisp
voices of the orange and gold
October leaves are laughing at death.

I want you to look beneath
the grass, to note
the fragile hieroglyphs
of ant, snail, beetle. I want
you to understand that you are
no more and no less necessary
than the brown recluse, the ruby-
throated hummingbird, the humpback
whale, the profligate mimosa.

I want to say, like Neruda,
that I am waiting for
"a great and common tenderness,"
that I still believe
we are capable of attention,
that anyone who notices the world
must want to save it.

*Hope for the
Future*

REBECCA BAGGETT

The Sky Never Ends

The sky

   never ends

      because

         God's still

            making it

TROYE-SUZANNE PLATT
AGE 6

We must believe small deeds matter, Great
Encourager, for You say mountains can be budged
with faith as small as mustard seeds. Ah, though,
there's nothing small about a Scottish hillside
blanketed with yellow mustard flowers. Tiny and
mighty—a package deal with You at our elbow.
Forgive us when we don't recognize mustard seed
power in changed lives, communities—within our
own hearts. Too often we wait for great, glitzy
flourishes and overlook tiny flickers of goodness.
They're all around, begging to be noticed and
gathered into a radiant harvest of hope.

MARGARET ANNE HUFFMAN

I Should Have,
I Could Have, I Will

I should have cried, hugged the woman,
given them money, bought everyone cake,
raised children, given blood,
written songs, danced, rescued baby birds,
swept broken glass from sidewalks,
learned first aid, become an EMT,
gone into the wars and stopped them.
With my arms wide open,
I should collect the children's guns
in a white sack, show them warm bread,
and green pushing through the dirt.
I could cover asphalt, whitewash
what's dirty, take away each ugly
thing I see, paint the streets blue,
the signs black, donate purple sheets
to the ambulances. I could
take you each in my arms. This time,
this time I will.

LAURA LEE WASHBURN

EVEN IF I KNEW

Even if I knew
   that tomorrow
the world would go to pieces,
I would still plant my apple tree.

MARTIN LUTHER
(1483–1546)

*Hope for the
Future*

THE TEST OF A FIRST-RATE INTELLIGENCE

The test of a first-rate intelligence is the ability
to hold two opposed ideas in mind at the same time
and still retain the ability to function.
One should, for example, be able to see that
things are hopeless and yet be determined
to make them better.

F. SCOTT FITZGERALD
(1896–1940)

DOVES IN SIGHT

In a world that sometimes seems bent on drowning
in its own misery, O God of Noah and second
chances, we're inspired by those who refuse to go
down for the count. Like Mother Teresa, Elie Wiesel
who was awarded the 1986 Nobel Prize for Peace,
and Candy Lightner who founded MADD; like
Gandhi and Martin Luther King and President
Jimmy Carter. They are Your doves, the
heroes/heroines who set out to carry only one small
message, do one small thing. Before you know it,
it's blossomed into something that makes a
difference . . . even if to only one person, one
situation. In that spirit, we'll become doves, too,
calling to one another visions of new land in sight.

MARGARET ANNE HUFFMAN

*Hope for the
Future*

In Spite of Everything

I keep my ideals,
because in spite of everything
I still believe that people
are really good at heart.

ANNE FRANK
(1929–1945)

Fourteen

INSPIRATION

THE BREEZE AT DAWN...

The breeze at dawn has secrets to tell you.
           Don't go back to sleep.
You must ask for what you really want.
           Don't go back to sleep.
People are going back and forth across the doorsill
           where the two worlds touch.
The door is round and open.
           Don't go back to sleep.

RUMI
(1207—1273)
TRANSLATED BY COLEMAN BARKS

DON'T DESTROY THE WORLD
(Excerpt)

Don't. Don't destroy the world.

I've never seen a flying fish.
I'm told they are orange
and I want to see: is it like melon or
rust or the harvest moon?
I want to hear their wings spread:
are they translucent?
and their leap.

I've never drunk hot brandy after
scooping snow angels in the blue twilight,
never wakened in the desert, in April
when the yucca is in citron bloom,
or felt the breath of whales
hot and moist on my face.

Inspiration

There was a time I
thought I couldn't take it: the bite of life.
I gunned the engine, swerved the winding road.
But I never say I *can't* any more. I can
take it. I want to take it all.

I want the future to extend before me like the horizon
widening as I walk. I want the blue sierra that I planted
squatting over the child in my womb
to grow into a thick tangled hedge
rich with blossoms and bees buzzing like a party.
I want the smell to make someone's
great great grandchild dizzy.

ELLEN BASS

Let Us Work

Therefore, let us work, let us develop all our
    possibilities;
not for ourselves, but for our fellow-creatures.
Let us be enlightened in our efforts,
let us strive after the general welfare of humanity
    and indeed of all creation.
We are born here to do certain things.
Life may be misery or not; it concerns us not;
let us do what we have to do. We are not here
    wholly alone
. . . we cannot save ourselves unless others are
    saved.
We cannot advance unless the general progress is
    assured.
We must help one another,
we must abandon our vulgar egocentric ideas,
we must expand ourselves so that the whole
    universe is identified with us,
and so that our interests are those of humanity.

188

Inspiration

SOYEN SHAKU
(1859–1919)

KEEP US, OH GOD, FROM PETTINESS

Keep us, Oh God, from pettiness; let us be large in
thought, in word, in deed.

Let us be done with fault-finding and leave off
self-seeking.

May we put away all pretense and meet each other
face to face—without self-pity and without
prejudice.

May we never be hasty in judgment and always
generous.

Let us take time for all things; make us to grow
calm, serene, gentle.

Teach us to put into action our better impulses,
straightforward and unafraid.

Grant that we may realize that it is the little
things that create differences, that in the big
things of life we are at one.

And may we strive to touch and to know the
great, common heart of us all, and, Oh Lord
God, let us forget not to be kind!

MARY STUART
(1878–1943)

Inspiration

For the Beauty of the Universe

Lord, may I be wakeful at sunrise to begin a new day for you, cheerful at sunset for having done my work for you; thankful at moonrise and under starshine for the beauty of the universe. And may I add what little may be in me to your great world.

THE ABBOT OF GREVE

What Really Matters

Oh Lord,

Make us aware that it is not the length of life
    that counts, but how it is lived that matters.

Teach us to understand that happiness is to be
    found not in what we have, but in what we are.

Open our eyes to the fact that the material things
    we enjoy come from you, who loaned them to
    us, and that we are not their real owners,
    but merely stewards.

Above all, teach us to know that to the extent
that we give, do we get back.

HARVEY M. HABER AND WAYNE R. ALLEN

Inspiration

KINDNESS

It is the history of our kindnesses
that alone makes this world tolerable.
If it were not for that,
for the effect of kind words,
kind looks, kind letters . . .
I should be inclined to think our life
a practical jest in the worst possible spirit.

ROBERT LOUIS STEVENSON
(1850—1894)

With the Heart of a Child

It's hard, serious work patching up this old world of ours, Lord of Giggling Children and Dancing Fish. We have our noses to the grindstone, shoulders to the plow and feet on the path. Yet all work and no play is dulling our vision and wearing us out. Remind us of the rejuvenation to be found from the sheer pleasure of playing and laughter that is so very good for heart, mind and soul. In the midst of all there is to do, send us out to skip in spring rains, run across beaches, grow a garden, and play in the snow.

MARGARET ANNE HUFFMAN

LET US BEGIN NOW

May the words you speak be gentle.
May you offer dreams that are soft.
May you grant wishes on crystal stars.
May you find promise in the morning sun.
May your days be filled with hope and strength.
Let us begin now to heal the world.

JUDITH A. LINDBERG

Inspiration

GO FORTH

Go forth in every direction—
        for the happiness, the harmony,
    the welfare of the many.
Offer your heart, the seeds of
        your own understanding
    like a lamp overturned
          and re-lit again
    illuminating the darkness.

THE BUDDHA

AUTHOR INDEX

PERMISSIONS AND
ACKNOWLEDGMENTS

Grateful acknowledgment is made to the authors and publishers for the use of the following material. Every effort has been made to contact original sources. If notified, the publishers will be pleased to rectify an omission in future editions.

Rebecca Baggett for "Testimony" and "What We Can Do."

Ballantine Books, a division of Random House Inc. for "Keep Us, Oh God, from Pettiness," by Mary Stuart from *The Beginning of Wisdom* by Thomas Becknell and Mary Ellen Ashcroft. Copyright © 1995 by Thomas Becknell and Mary Ellen Ashcroft. Reprinted by permission of Ballantine Books, a division of Random House Inc.

Bantam Doubleday Dell Publishing Group Inc. for "Friendship" by Dinah Maria Mulock Craig, for "Trees" by Joyce Kilmer, and for "New Friends and Old Friends" by Joseph Parry from *Poems That Touch the Heart,* edited by A. L. Alexander. Copyright © 1941, 1956 by Doubleday, a division of Bantam Doubleday Dell Publishing Group Inc.

Coleman Barks for "The Guest House," "Hundreds of Ways," "In Your Light I Learn How to Love," and "Sublime Generosity" from *The Essential Rumi,* translated by Coleman Barks and John Moyne. Copyright © 1995. Permission to reprint granted by Coleman Barks.

Virginia Barrett for "If Love Takes Shape."

Ellen Bass for "Don't Destroy the World."

Richard Beban for "On Guardian Angels."

James Bertolino for "To Think Like a Planet."

Mike W. Blottenberger for "The Soul Has No Color."

Gayle Brandeis for "The Body Politic of Peace."

Janine Canan for "The Golden Arrow."

Richard Carlson for "Did I Fill My Life with Love?" from *Handbook for the Heart,* edited by Richard Carlson and Benjamin Shield. Copyright © 1993 by Richard Carlson and Benjamin Shield. Published by Little, Brown and Company. Reprinted with permission by Richard Carlson.

Chariot Victor Publishing for "A Child's Prayer for Peace" by Josephine Davies from *Prayers for a Fragile World,* written and compiled by Carol Watson, copyright © 1991 by Lion Publishing; and for "Love One Another" from *365 Children's Prayers,* edited by Carol Watson, copyright © 1989 by Lion Publishing. Reprinted by permission of Chariot Victor Publishing.

Lukas Jai Clary for "Remembrance."

Ralph S. Coleman for "Wild Strawberries."

Continuum Publishing for "Waking Up" by Thich Nhat Hanh from *The Gift of Prayer,* by Fellowship in Prayer. Copyright © 1995 by Fellowship in Prayer. Reprinted with the permission of The Continuum Publishing Company.

Barbara Crooker for "Walking Alone on a Thickly Starred Night."

Marylisa W. DeDomenicis for "Simply Put."

Denise A. DeWald for "Guard Me from Destructive Thoughts" and "Homeless."

Corrine De Winter for "Little Lives" and "Sylvan."

Ida Fasel for "Stopping by a Candy Shelf."

Maureen Tolman Flannery for "Challenge to the Child" and "Forestry."

Sam Hamill for "I Make My Home in the Mountains" by Li Po, translated from the Chinese by Sam Hamill, from *Banished Immortal: Visions of Li T'ai-Po* by Sam Hamill. Copyright © 1987. Reprinted with permission of the translator.

Maryanne Hannan for "A Reflection."

Harcourt Brace & Company for "The Peace of Wild Things" from *Openings,* copyright © 1968 and renewed 1996 by Wendell Berry. Reprinted by permission of Harcourt Brace & Company.

HarperCollins Publishers for "A Sense of Wonder" from *The Sense of Wonder* by Rachel Carson. Copyright © 1956 by Rachel Carson. Copyright © renewed 1984 by Roger Christie. Reprinted with permission by HarperCollins Publishers Inc.

HarperCollins Publishers for "Send Us Out" by Sheila Cassidy from *Laughter, Silence and Shouting* by Kathy Keay. Copyright © 1994. Reprinted by permission from HarperCollins Publishers Ltd., London.

HarperCollins Publishers for "May I Be a Protector" from *The Tibetan Book of Living and Dying* by Sogyal Rinpoche. Copyright © 1993 by Rigpa Fellowship. Reprinted by permission of HarperCollins Publishers Inc.

Hazelden Foundation for "Letting Go" by Stephanie Kaza, "Lost" by David Wagoner, and "On Paths That Have Heart" by Carlos Castaneda from *Lighting a Candle,* edited by Molly Young Brown. Copyright © 1994 by Hazelden. Reprinted with permission by Hazelden Foundation, Center City, MN.

C. David Hay for "Wind Song."

Margaret Anne Huffman for "Caught on the Barb," "Deliver Us from Jumping to Conclusions," "Doves In Sight," "The Joy of Coming Unstuck," "Reaping Mustard Seed Hope," and "With the Heart of a Child."

Rick Kempa for "Whatever She Invites."

Alfred A. Knopf Inc. for "Litany" from *Collected Poems* by Langston Hughes. Copyright © 1995 by the Estate of Langston Hughes. Reprinted by permission of Alfred A. Knopf Inc.

Shirley Kobar for "The Sun."

Rabbi Harold Kushner for "To Love and Be Loved" from *Handbook for the Heart,* edited by Richard Carlson and Benjamin Shield. Copyright © 1993 by Richard Carlson and Benjamin Shield. Published by Little, Brown and Company. Reprinted with permission by Richard Carlson.

Elizabeth Searle Lamb for "So Must Peace Come."

Arlene Gay Levine for "Affair in the Garden" and "Ode to the Rain."

Judith A. Lindberg for "Let Us Begin Now."

Little, Brown and Company for "Sleeping in the Forest" from *Twelve Moons* by Mary Oliver. Copyright © 1978 by Mary Oliver. First appeared in *The Ohio Review.* Reprinted with permission by the publisher, Little, Brown and Company.

Louisiana State University Press for "Natural Theology" by Kelly Cherry from *Natural Theology* by Kelly Cherry. Copyright © 1988 by Kelly Cherry. Reprinted with permission by Louisiana State University Press.

Patricia Love for "Kicking and Screaming into the Classroom" from *Handbook for the Heart,* edited by Richard Carlson and Benjamin Shield. Copyright © 1993 by Richard Carlson and Benjamin Shield. Published by Little, Brown and Company. Reprinted with permission by Richard Carlson.

Loveline Books for "Prayer for Humanity" from *Handbook to Higher Consciousness* by Ken Keyes Jr. Copyright © 1975 by Living Love Center. Reprinted with permission by Loveline Books.

Lutterworth Press of Parkwest Publishing Inc. for "I Was Wrong—Forgive Me" from *Lord of Time* by Frank Topping.

William Morrow and Company for "A Great Secret" by Albert Camus and "The Potentiality of the Human Race" by James Agee, from *May All Be Fed: Diet for a New World* by John Robbins. Copyright © 1992. Reprinted with permission by William Morrow and Company.

New Directions Publishing Corp. for "Saints" by Thomas Merton from *New Seeds of Contemplation.* Copyright © 1961 by The Abbey of Gethsemani Inc. Reprinted by permission of New Directions Publishing Corp.

Julia Older for "Combinations."

Parallax Press for "The True Meaning of Compassion" by Joanna Macy. Reprinted from *World As Lover, World As Self* by Joanna Macy with permission of Parallax Press, Berkeley, California.

George Perreault for "One at a Time."

Troye-Suzanne Platt for "The Sky Never Ends."

S. Ramnath for "Star Conversations."

Random House for "How to End War?" by Jack Riemer from *When Bad Things Happen to Good People* by Harold S. Kushner. Copyright © 1981, 1989 by Harold S. Kushner. Reprinted by permission of Schocken Books, distributed by Pantheon Books, a division of Random House Inc.

Thomas L. Reid for "A Silent Certainty."

Fleming H. Revell, a division of Baker Book House Company, for "Prayer for a World Vision" from *The Prayers of Peter Marshall,* edited by Catherine Marshall. Copyright © 1954. Reprinted with permission.

Elisavietta Ritchie for "For a Certain Artist."

Linda Goodman Robiner for "Prayer."

Kate Robinson for "All."

Blanche Rosloff for "A Fresh Dream."

Nancy Rustici for "God."

Rabbi Rami M. Shapiro for "Distinction," "Peace," "Sabbath of Forgiveness," and "Unending Love."

Meredith Sabini for "Please Print Legibly."

Hilda Sanderson for "Advice" and "Prayer of This Imperfect Me."

Ralph Schillace for "Somewhere in a Small Village."

The Albert Schweitzer Institute for "Reverence for Life" and "True Happiness." Reprinted with permission of The Albert Schweitzer Institute, 700 Christian Street, Wallingford, CT 06492.

Self-Counsel Press for "What Really Matters" from *Giving Thanks* by Harvey M. Haber and Wayne R. Allen. Self-Counsel Press, copyright © 1994. Used by permission.

Sherman Asher Publishing for "River" from *Lizard Light: Poems from the Earth* by Penny Harter. Copyright © 1998 by Penny Harter. Reprinted by permission of Sherman Asher Publishing.

Bernie Siegel for "Simply Being Loved" from *Handbook for the Heart,* edited by Richard Carlson and Benjamin Shield. Copyright © 1993 by Richard Carlson and